The Divine Chronicles

Of

LORD JAGANNATH

Sutapa Saha

CONTENTS

ACKNOWLEDGMENTS

With heartfelt gratitude, I extend my sincerest appreciation to everyone who supported and guided me throughout the creation of **The Divine Chronicles of Lord Jagannath**. This book is the result of countless hours of devotion, research, and writing, and it would not have been possible without the love and encouragement of those around me.

First and foremost, I am profoundly grateful to Lord Jagannath himself, whose divine presence inspired each page of this book. This work is my humble offering to him, and I am ever thankful for the grace and blessings that sustained me throughout this journey.

I extend my deepest thanks to my family, who stood by me with unwavering support, patience, and love, encouraging me at every step of this creative journey. Their belief in me and their constant words of encouragement kept me focused and motivated.

A special note of gratitude goes to my mentors and teachers who imparted their wisdom and guidance, deepening my understanding of mythology and devotion. Their insights enriched the stories and gave them a profound spiritual depth.

Finally, to the readers and devotees who will open these pages—thank you. This book is for you. May these stories of Lord Jagannath touch your heart as they have touched mine, and may his blessings be with you alway.

Sutapa Saha

INTRODUCTION

In the sacred lands of India, where mythology intertwines with the fabric of daily life, the stories of Lord Jagannath stand as timeless testimonies of divine grace, devotion, and transformation. Lord Jagannath, the Supreme Lord of Puri, is not only revered for his divine form but also for his boundless compassion that transcends barriers of space, time, and circumstance. He is the embodiment of mercy, fulfilling the deepest wishes of his devotees, guiding them from the paths of doubt to the shores of faith, from pride to humility, and ultimately, from the cycle of birth and death to the eternal embrace of liberation.

This collection of ten stories brings to life the miraculous tales of devotion and divine intervention surrounding Lord Jagannath. Each tale reflects a unique journey, a personal transformation, and the profound spiritual connection between the devotee and the Lord. From the humble servant who offers a gift of love, to the intellectual scholar who learns the value of humility, to the fervent seeker who is granted the ultimate liberation—these stories remind us that the Lord sees beyond the surface and responds to the sincerity of one's heart.

In these pages, you will encounter characters from various walks of life: the hunchback tailor whose devotion to Lord Jagannath transcends physical limitations, the scholarly Odian Acharya whose pride is shattered by the grace of the Lord, and the determined Ganapati Bhat who travels from Karnataka to Puri in search of spiritual fulfillment. Each of them has a moment of reckoning with Lord Jagannath, and in that moment, their lives are forever changed.

The stories contained within this book are not just about miraculous events or divine interventions; they are also about the power of faith, the importance of humility, and the unyielding grace of a Lord who is ever-present, waiting for his devotees to come with open hearts and sincere prayers. They are an invitation to embrace the divine, to seek the Lord not with expectations but with love, and to understand that true liberation comes from surrendering to his will.

As you journey through these stories, may you be inspired by the devotion, humility, and faith of the characters, and may Lord Jagannath's divine presence touch your heart in ways both profound and beautiful.

CHAPTER 1

THE DIVINE TEST

OF

DEVOTION

Sutapa Saha

KING PURUSHOTTAM DEV AND THE BLESSINGS OF LORD JAGANNATH

In the illustrious Ganga dynasty, there lived a noble and devout king named Purushottam Dev. His reign was marked by justice, devotion, and a deep love for Lord Jagannath, the presiding deity of Puri. His faith in the Lord guided every action he took, and it was this devotion that shaped his destiny in unexpected ways.

One day, King Purushottam Dev visited the kingdom of Kanchi, where he met King Kanchi's daughter, Princess Padmavati. The moment he saw her, he was captivated by her beauty, grace, and above all, her deep devotion to the divine. Her piety and kindness resonated with his own spiritual values, and he knew she was the one he wished to marry. With great respect, he asked the King of Kanchi for her hand in marriage. The Kanchi king, recognizing Purushottam Dev's virtue, agreed and was pleased to see his daughter wed to such a devout king.

However, as part of the marriage preparations, the Kanchi king sent his minister to Puri to observe Purushottam Dev's kingdom and ensure that his daughter would be well cared for in her new home. When the minister arrived, it was the time of the grand Rath Yatra, a festival where Lord Jagannath, along with his siblings Balabhadra and Subhadra, are taken out in a chariot procession. It is a tradition during this festival for the King of Puri to sweep the road before the chariots with a golden broom, symbolizing his humility and service to the Lord.

The minister, witnessing this, was shocked. He saw the king sweeping the streets and perceived it as demeaning for a king to perform the duties of a sweeper. Returning to Kanchi, he advised the king against the marriage, expressing concern that Purushottam Dev's role as a "sweeper" was unbecoming of a king who would marry their princess. Influenced by this, the Kanchi king decided to cancel the marriage and arranged a swayamvara (a traditional ceremony in ancient India where princess can choose her husband) for

Princess Padmavati, inviting all the eligible kings—
except Purushottam Dev.

When Purushottam Dev learned of this insult, he
was deeply offended. The Kanchi king had broken
his promise and insulted his devotion to Lord
Jagannath. Enraged, Purushottam Dev vowed to
teach the Kanchi king a lesson and declared war on
the kingdom of Kanchi. Before the battle began,
both sides agreed on a wager: if Kanchi won, they
would take the idols of Jagannath, Balabhadra, and
Subhadra from Puri and place them behind their
Ganesh deity, worshiping them in that order. If
Purushottam Dev won, he could place the Ganesh
idol behind the Jagannath idols in Puri.

The war began, but on the first day, Purushottam
Dev's forces faced severe setbacks. Their camp was
ravaged by fire, and many soldiers were injured,
forcing them to retreat. Troubled by the events,
Purushottam Dev prayed earnestly to Lord
Jagannath, expressing his fear that if he lost, the
Lord's idols would be dishonored by being placed
behind Ganesh. "How can you, the Lord of all, be
placed behind your devotee Ganesh?" he pleaded.

That night, Lord Jagannath appeared in the king's
dream and reassured him, saying, "Do not worry,
my devotee Purushottam. I, along with my brother
Balabhadra, will lead your army tomorrow. We will
fight as soldiers by your side, and victory shall be

yours." The Lord also promised that Purushottam Dev would know of their presence by a divine sign.

The next day, as the battle resumed, two young warriors, one dark-skinned riding a dark horse and the other fair-skinned on a white horse, led the charge. Their presence energized the army, and they fought with unmatched vigor. As they passed through a village, they became thirsty and saw a woman named Manika carrying buttermilk. The two warriors drank two full pots of buttermilk in an instant and, having no money to pay, gave Manika a ring with the inscription "Jai Jagannath" on it, instructing her to show it to the king for payment.

When King Purushottam Dev arrived at the spot, Manika showed him the ring. Recognizing it as a divine token from Lord Jagannath, he understood that the Lord and Lord Balabhadra themselves had led his army. Overwhelmed with gratitude, he rewarded Manika with riches and renamed the village "Manikapatnam" in her honor.

With the divine presence on his side, Purushottam Dev's army crushed the forces of Kanchi. The Kanchi king, realizing his folly, surrendered, and Purushottam Dev claimed victory. The condition of placing the Ganesh idol behind the Jagannath idols was met, and the king of Kanchi agreed to give his daughter Padmavati's hand in marriage to Purushottam Dev.

However, still hurt by the earlier insult, Purushottam Dev ordered his minister to find a sweeper to marry Princess Padmavati. The princess, heartbroken by these words, waited patiently, trusting that time would heal the king's wounds.

A year later, during the Rath Yatra, as Purushottam Dev once again performed the ceremonial sweeping with the golden broom, the minister approached him and reminded him of his previous command. "My king," he said, "you asked me to find a suitable sweeper for Princess Padmavati. I have found him. Who could be more worthy than you, who serves the Lord so humbly?"

Purushottam Dev, his anger long cooled, smiled at the minister's words. He recognized the truth in them and, with a heart full of grace, agreed to marry Princess Padmavati. The marriage was celebrated with great joy, and Princess Padmavati became the beloved queen of Puri.

Thus, the story of King Purushottam Dev and Lord Jagannath became a timeless tale of devotion, humility, and divine intervention, reminding all that true kingship lies in service to the divine.

Two young warriors drank buttermilk, and gave Manika a
ring with inscription "Jai Jagannath".

CHAPTER 2

THE VANISHING SAINT

12

RAMANUJACHARYA'S MYSTICAL JOURNEY WITH LORD JAGANNATH

In the heart of the sacred town of Puri, Odisha where the grand temple of Lord Jagannath stands, an extraordinary event unfolded that demonstrated the divine will of the Lord and his unique relationship with his devotees.

Sripad Ramanujacharya, the revered saint and philosopher from South India, had earned a reputation for his deep devotion, knowledge, and strict adherence to the rituals of deity worship. His teachings and practices were followed with great discipline across many temples in the southern part of India. One day, driven by his desire to pay homage to the great Lord Jagannath, Ramanujacharya embarked on a pilgrimage to Puri.

Upon reaching the Jagannath Temple, Ramanujacharya observed the daily rituals and offerings made by the temple priests. However, as he watched, he became increasingly concerned. The rituals performed by the priests seemed disorderly to him, not adhering to the strict and meticulous procedures that he was accustomed to in the South. The offerings, the manner of worship, and even the timing of certain rituals did not align with the strict codes of temple worship as he knew them.

Ramanujacharya, being a person of great piety and knowledge, felt it was his duty to correct what he perceived as errors in the worship of Lord Jagannath. He approached the King of Puri with respect and humility, expressing his concerns. "O King," he said, "I have observed that the way the priests are conducting the worship of Lord Jagannath does not follow the correct and disciplined procedures. The rituals are not being performed according to the strict rules that should be observed in the worship of such a great deity. If you allow, I will teach the priests the proper methods so that the worship of Lord Jagannath is done in the most reverent and correct way."

The King, deeply respecting Ramanujacharya's wisdom and reputation, agreed to his proposal. He issued a royal decree that the temple priests were to undergo training under Ramanujacharya, starting from the very next day. The priests, though devoted and sincere in their service, felt saddened by this decision. They had always believed that their way of serving the Lord, passed down through generations, was pleasing to Lord Jagannath. Now, with Ramanujacharya's intervention, they began to doubt themselves and wondered if they had somehow displeased the Lord.

That night, the priests prayed fervently to Lord Jagannath, pouring out their hearts and seeking reassurance. They expressed their sorrow and asked the Lord if they had indeed been serving Him incorrectly all this time.

The next morning, as the sun rose and the time for the training approached, the priests with heavy heart gathered in the temple, awaiting the arrival of Ramanujacharya. But as time passed, there was no sign of the great saint. Hours went by, and the priests, along with the king, grew increasingly concerned. They searched for Ramanujacharya everywhere—in the house where he had been staying, in the temple, and throughout the town of Puri. But he was nowhere to be found.

The people of Puri were perplexed. How could such a great and punctual saint simply vanish? As the search continued, news arrived from Kurma Kshetra, a sacred place in South India. To everyone's astonishment, it was discovered that Ramanujacharya had awakened that very morning in Kurma Kshetra, far from Puri.

Confused and surprised, Ramanujacharya himself was unsure how he had ended up back in South India overnight. As he prayed and meditated, seeking answers, Lord Jagannath appeared before him in a vision. The Lord, with a gentle and compassionate smile, said to Ramanujacharya,"Oh Ramanuja, I am pleased with your devotion and your desire to ensure that I am worshiped properly. But know this—each place and each tradition has its own way of serving Me, and I find joy in all sincere offerings made with love and devotion. In Puri, I have my own unique ways, and the way the priests here serve Me is exactly how I desire. It is out of love for them and their service that I brought you back to Kurma Kshetra. There is no need for any change in Puri. My will is that the traditions there continue as they are."

Ramanujacharya, humbled and moved by the Lord's words, realized the depth of Lord Jagannath's love for His devotees and their unique ways of worship. He understood that the Lord's pleasure does not lie in the strictness of rituals but in the devotion and love with which they are performed.

With a heart full of reverence, Ramanujacharya bowed to Lord Jagannath and accepted the divine will. He returned to his work in South India, carrying with him a profound lesson in humility and the boundless love of the Lord for His devotees.

Thus, the priests of Puri continued their service to Lord Jagannath with renewed joy, knowing that their ways were beloved by the Lord. The story of Ramanujacharya's visit to Puri became a cherished tale, reminding all that true worship is not about rigid adherence to rituals but about the love and devotion that flows from the heart.

Lord Jagannath talking to Ramanujacharya, about his divine
will.

CHAPTER 3

THE STRIKES THAT VANISHED

Sutapa Saha

A LESSON FROM LORD JAGANNATH ON UNWAVERING FAITH

In a quaint village near Puri lived Arjun Mishra, a devout and learned pundit known for his unwavering faith in Lord Jagannath. Arjun Mishra was not just a scholar; he was known as "Geeta Panda" because of his deep devotion to the teachings of the Bhagavad Gita. Every day, he spent hours reciting slokas from the sacred text, particularly cherishing the verse from Chapter 9, Verse 22: "Ananyāś chintayanto māṁ ye janāḥ paryupāsate, teṣāṁ nityābhiyuktānāṁ yoga-kṣhemaṁ vahāmyaham." ("To those who are constantly devoted and who worship Me with love, I give them the understanding by which they can come to Me.")

Arjun Mishra believed this verse with all his heart, trusting that Lord Jagannath would take care of all his needs. He led a simple life, never did he worried about material wealth or even daily sustenance. Whatever little food came to him as alms, he accepted with gratitude, sharing it with his family and praising the Lord for His provision.

However, life was not easy for his wife. She struggled with the meager food and resources they had, and often, there wasn't enough to go around.

Despite her devotion, she couldn't help but worry about their future. Every time she expressed her concerns to Arjun Mishra, he would point to the verse in the Bhagavad Gita and reassure her, saying, "The Lord will provide for us. We just need to have trust in Him."

One day, overwhelmed by frustration, his wife took the Bhagavad Gita and struck through the verse in Chapter 9, Verse 22, with her pen, not once but three times. "Let's see how the Lord will provide now," she thought, feeling guilty yet desperate.

The next day, as Arjun Mishra was out, there was a knock on the door. When his wife opened it, she saw two young boys standing there. They were strikingly handsome—one with a dark complexion and the other fair. Both had a divine aura around them. The boys were carrying a large basket brimming with food items, enough to feed the family for days.

The boys spoke kindly, "Mother, is this the house of Geeta Panda? We have brought *prasad* (Lord's food offerings) for you and your family."

Surprised, Arjun Mishra's wife asked how they knew her husband. The boys replied with a smile, "We are his disciples, and we have come to offer our *Guru Dakshina* (an offering for teacher)."

Overwhelmed by their generosity, she invited them inside, "Please, come in and rest. You must be tired from carrying such a heavy basket. Stay and share this *prasad* with us."

But the boys declined, saying, "We cannot eat, for we have ulcers on our tongues."

Concerned, she asked to see their tongues. When they opened their mouths, she was astonished to see three distinct strike marks across their tongues—the exact same marks she had made in the Bhagavad Gita.

Before she could react, the boys left, leaving the basket behind. When Arjun Mishra returned home, his wife was overjoyed and began to praise him, "You didn't tell me that you had taken up teaching! Your students brought so much *prasad* for us, we could never finish it all!"

Confused, Arjun Mishra asked her to explain. As she recounted the story and mentioned the three strike marks on their tongues, Arjun Mishra realized what had happened. Without saying a word, he hurried to his room and opened the Bhagavad Gita. To his amazement, the strikes his wife had made on the sacred verse were gone, as if they had never been there.

Tears filled Arjun Mishra's eyes as he turned to his wife, "See, you doubted the Lord, but He Himself came to our aid. Those boys were none other than Lord Jagannath and his brother, Lord Balabhadra. They brought us this food to show you that His promise in the Bhagavad Gita is true. He takes care of those who have unwavering faith in Him."

Ashamed and filled with remorse, Arjun Mishra's wife understood the depth of the Lord's love and care. The family immediately rushed to the Lord Jagannath's Temple, where they offered their heartfelt prayers of gratitude and sought forgiveness from the Lord.

From that day onward, Arjun Mishra's wife never doubted the Lord's provision. The story of Arjun Mishra and the divine visit of Lord Jagannath spread throughout the village, becoming a timeless lesson in faith and devotion. The villagers, inspired by the tale, often recited the sacred verse from the Bhagavad Gita, reminding themselves that the Lord always takes care of those who trust in Him with all their heart.

Lord Jagannath and Lord Balabhadra standing infront of
Pundit Arjun Mishra's house with food baskets

CHAPTER 4

THE WHALE

AND

THE DEVOTEE

Sutapa Saha

A STORY OF FAITH AND SALVATION AT SEA

Captain Beetle, a seasoned sailor from France, was known for his courage and skill at sea. He had weathered many storms and braved countless dangers during his voyages. One day, while sailing through the Bay of Bengal, he and his crew found themselves facing one of the most terrifying challenges of their lives.

The day had started with ominous clouds gathering on the horizon, and soon, a fierce storm erupted. The once calm sea turned violent, with massive waves crashing against the ship, threatening to upturn it. The wind howled like a wild beast, and the ship creaked under the immense pressure of the storm. To make matters worse, as they struggled to keep the ship afloat, Captain Beetle spotted a massive whale approaching them, riding the crest of a towering wave. The whale was so enormous that it seemed capable of engulfing the entire ship in one mighty gulp.

Panic spread among the crew like wildfire. The sailors, despite their experience, were gripped with fear, knowing that their chances of survival were slim. Captain Beetle himself, though always composed, felt a deep sense of dread. He knew that the storm, the raging sea, and the looming threat of the whale could spell disaster. In the heart of the tempest, he found himself silently praying for a miracle, hoping against hope that something would change the course of events.

Amidst the chaos, Captain Beetle noticed something strange. One of the passengers, a man who had been silent throughout the voyage, sat calmly in a corner, his eyes fixed on a small picture of Lord Jagannath that he held in his hands. Unlike everyone else on board, this man showed no signs of fear or anxiety. His face was serene, as if he were completely untouched by the turmoil around him.

Curious and desperate for answers, Captain Beetle approached the man. "Aren't you afraid?" he asked, unable to comprehend how anyone could remain so calm in such a terrifying situation. "How can you sit there so peacefully while the rest of us are on the brink of disaster?"

The man looked up at the captain and smiled. "Why should I worry?" he replied. "When Lord Jagannath can carry us across the vast ocean of life, what is this small sea? My faith is in Him, and I know He will protect us."

The captain, though not a believer in the same faith, was moved by the man's conviction. Desperation pushed him to ask, "Can you pray to your Lord Jagannath? And ask Him to save us from this whale and this storm."

Without hesitation, the devotee closed his eyes and prayed with all his heart, asking Lord Jagannath to protect them and divert the whale from its path. As he prayed, Captain Beetle watched in awe as, just a short distance from the ship, the giant whale suddenly veered off course. It changed direction, swimming away from the ship as if guided by some unseen force. The crew gasped in astonishment, unable to believe what they had just witnessed.

The captain, still shaken but filled with a newfound hope, turned to the devotee once more. "Please, ask your Lord to calm the sea so that we may reach the shore safely."

The devotee nodded and prayed again, this time asking Lord Jagannath to calm the storm and the raging sea. As the captain and crew watched in wonder, a bolt of lightning flashed across the sky, and almost immediately, the waves began to subside. The wind lost its fury, and the sea, which had been so wild just moments before, became as calm as a placid lake.

Captain Beetle could hardly believe his eyes. The storm had passed, the sea was calm, and their ship, though battered, was safe. With a heart full of gratitude and disbelief, he steered the ship towards the nearest shore. The crew, too, were filled with awe, realizing that they had just witnessed something beyond their understanding.

When Captain Beetle finally returned to France, he could not keep the story to himself. He spoke of the great miracle that had saved them in the Bay of Bengal, and how the prayers of a humble devotee of Lord Jagannath had calmed the sea and diverted a giant whale. The tale of Lord Jagannath's divine intervention spread far and wide, and many who heard it were moved by the power of faith.

Captain Beetle, though from a different land and faith, always remembered that day as the day he witnessed the mercy and power of Lord Jagannath. He never forgot the calmness of the devotee who trusted in his Lord, and he carried that memory with him for the rest of his life, forever grateful for the miracle that had saved him and his crew.

The giant whale riding the crest of a towering wave, ready to engulf the entire ship in one mighty gulp.

Sutapa Saha

CHAPTER 5

THE KING'S TEST

AND

THE LORD'S MERCY

Sutapa Saha

THE MIRACLE OF JAGANNATH'S HAIR

Talicha Mahapatra was a devoted servant of Lord Jagannath in Puri, known for his deep faith and unwavering dedication. Every day, he took great pleasure in serving the Lord, particularly in adorning Him with beautiful flowers, jewellery, and garlands. Talicha's love for the Lord was so intense that he would often forget himself in his service, feeling that his every breath belonged to Lord Jagannath.

One day, the king of Puri decided to visit the Jagannath Temple unexpectedly, without prior notice to the temple priests. The visit of the king was always a grand affair, and the priests would usually prepare meticulously for it. However, this time, the king's sudden arrival caught everyone off guard. The priests hurriedly began their rituals, trying to ensure that everything was perfect for the royal visit.

As Talicha Mahapatra was preparing for the king's arrival, he realized with horror that he had forgotten to bring a garland for Lord Jagannath. The king had already entered the temple, and there was no time to fetch one. In a moment of desperation, Talicha decided to remove the garland he was wearing around his own neck and place it on the Lord. He knew that this was a personal garland, but his devotion and love for the Lord made him feel that offering it to Lord Jagannath was the right thing to do then.

When the king came to offer his prayers, he was deeply moved by the sight of Lord Jagannath adorned with such beauty. As was the custom, the priest then took the garland from the deity and placed it around the neck of the king as a blessing. The king gratefully accepted the garland, but as he was about to leave, he noticed something unusual—a long strand of hair caught in the garland.

The king's face darkened as he realized what must have happened. He turned to Talicha Mahapatra and asked sternly, "Are you sure this garland was Lord Jagannath's?"

Talicha, though internally terrified, replied, "Yes, my lord, it is the garland of Lord Jagannath Himself."

The king's suspicion grew. "If this garland belongs to Lord Jagannath, how could there be a hair in it? The deity has no hair!" The king's tone was accusatory, and Talicha could feel the weight of the situation pressing down on him.

Inwardly, Talicha was frightened, knowing that if the king were to discover the truth, it would lead to severe punishment. Yet, his devotion and faith in Lord Jagannath gave him the courage to maintain his statement. "My king, this is indeed the hair of Lord Jagannath," he repeated, trusting that the Lord would protect him.

The king, now determined to uncover the truth, announced, "Tomorrow, I will come to the temple and inspect the deity myself to see if Lord Jagannath has hair."

That night, Talicha Mahapatra was filled with anxiety. He prayed fervently to Lord Jagannath, pleading with Him to save him from the king's wrath. Talicha knew he had acted out of pure devotion, but he also knew that the king might not see it that way.

As Talicha prayed, he eventually drifted off to sleep, where Lord Jagannath appeared to him in a dream. The Lord, with a gentle smile, assured him, "Do not worry, Talicha. I will protect you. Tomorrow, when the king arrives, you will find that I indeed have hair. Trust in Me."

The next morning, Talicha awoke with a mixture of relief and apprehension. He rushed to the temple, eager to see if the Lord's words would come true. To his astonishment, when he checked the deity of Lord Jagannath, he found long, silky strands of hair flowing from the head of the deity. Talicha was overwhelmed with gratitude and awe at the Lord's divine intervention.

When the king arrived at the temple, Talicha confidently invited him to inspect the deity. The king, still skeptical, approached the deity and was shocked to see the long, flowing hair on the head of Lord Jagannath. He was convinced that Talicha had somehow attached fake hair to the deity's head, so he decided to test it further.

"Is this real hair?" the king asked, eyeing Talicha closely.

Talicha, with unshaken faith, replied, "My king, please check for yourself."

The king reached out and gently tugged at one of the strands of hair. To his amazement, the hair came away in his hand, and as it did, he saw a small drop of blood appear on the deity's head where the hair had been pulled. The king's eyes widened in disbelief. This was no trick—this was a miracle!

Immediately, the king fell to his knees, deeply humbled and filled with reverence. "Forgive me, Lord," he whispered, his voice choking with emotion. "Forgive me, Talicha, for doubting your devotion and the sanctity of our Lord."

When the king raised his eyes to look at the deity once more, he was stunned to see that the hair had vanished. The deity of Lord Jagannath stood as He always did, serene and without hair. The king understood that this was a divine play, a "leela" of Lord Jagannath, to protect His devotee and to demonstrate that He is always present in the lives of those who loved Him.

The king, filled with newfound respect and humility, asked Talicha Mahapatra for forgiveness. He recognized the depth of Talicha's devotion and the greatness of Lord Jagannath's mercy. From that day on, the king never doubted the power of Lord Jagannath or the sincerity of His devotees.

Talicha Mahapatra continued his service to the Lord with even greater devotion, knowing that Lord Jagannath was always watching over him. The story of Talicha Mahapatra and the miracle of Lord Jagannath's hair became a cherished tale in Puri, a testament to the Lord's boundless love and protection for His devotees.

King was shocked to see Lord Jagannath's hair, suspected
Talicha of deception, and decided to test the truth.

CHAPTER 6

THE DIVINE PENANCE

Sutapa Saha

WHEN LORD JAGANNATH TRANSFORMED FIRE INTO FLOWERS

King Kulashekhara was a revered ruler, known not only for his wisdom and dedication to his kingdom but also for his profound devotion to Lord Jagannath. His days were filled with the responsibilities of governance, ensuring the prosperity and welfare of his subjects. However, no matter how busy he was, Kulashekhara always made time to immerse himself in spiritual activities, particularly listening to Hari Katha—stories and teachings about Lord Krishna and His devotees.

One day, a highly respected Guru arrived at the court. King Kulashekhara, ever humble and devoted, immediately descended from his throne, prostrated himself before the Guru in a full Sashtang Pranam (a prostration with all eight limbs touching the ground), and respectfully seated the Guru on an elevated seat. The Guru's presence filled the court with a divine aura, and the proceedings continued as usual.

As the Guru began to speak, a small fly buzzed into the court and landed on the king's forehead, right where the dust from his earlier prostration lay. Without thinking, King Kulashekhara instinctively raised his hand to shoo the fly away, inadvertently wiping away the dust from his forehead. The Guru, observing this, shook his head subtly in disapproval.

King Kulashekhara noticed the Guru's expression and, concerned that whether he had made a mistake, respectfully inquired, "Gurudev, have I done something wrong?"

The Guru, with a heavy heart, responded, "My dear king, the dust you wiped away was no ordinary dust. It was the sacred blessing you received from bowing before me, capable of cleansing your lifetimes of sin. By removing it, you symbolically rejected the purification it offered. Now, the sins you have accumulated over your many lives may no longer be absolved in this one."

Saying this, the Guru stood up and left the court, leaving the king in a state of deep despair. King Kulashekhara was devastated, feeling as though he had committed a grave offense. Determined to make amends, he summoned all the learned pundits and scholars in his kingdom, asking them to find a way for him to atone for his mistake.

After much deliberation and study of the scriptures, the pundits discovered a severe penance that could purify the king of his sins. They informed the king, "Your Majesty, there is a way to atone, but it is an extremely difficult and painful process. You must perform 108 Sashtang Pranams on a copper plate that is 12 feet long, 3 feet wide, and 6 centimeters thick. This plate must be heated until it is red hot and placed above a bed of burning coals. Only then will you be cleansed of your sins."

The king listened attentively, and without hesitation, he declared, "I will perform this penance, no matter the difficulty. I must seek forgiveness from my Guru and be purified of my sins."

The ministers, nobles, and subjects were horrified by the prospect. They pleaded with the king to reconsider, fearing for his life. "Your Majesty," they said, "you are our protector and guide. If you harm yourself in this way, who will care for the kingdom? Please, find another way."

But King Kulashekhara was resolute. "I have caused my Guru pain, and I must atone for it in the manner prescribed by the scriptures. Prepare the copper plate."

The ministers had no choice but to comply with the king's wishes. The copper plate was prepared according to the instructions, and a great crowd gathered to witness the king's penance. The heat from the plate was so intense that even standing near it was unbearable, yet the king, with unwavering faith, approached it calmly.

As King Kulashekhara performed the first Sashtang Pranam on the red-hot plate, his skin immediately began to burn, and his flesh sizzled. The pain was excruciating, but the king endured it without complaint, his mind focused solely on seeking forgiveness.

The people, seeing their beloved king suffer, began to weep and pray fervently to Lord Jagannath. "O Lord Jagannath," they cried, "please protect our king, your devoted servant! He has been a righteous ruler and a great devotee. Do not let him suffer like this!"

Just as the king prepared to perform his second prostration, a Brahman appeared in the crowd. He was a striking figure, radiating a divine presence. The Brahman approached the king and said, "O King Kulasekhara, there are other ways to atone for your sins. You need not subject yourself to such extreme suffering."

The king, though in immense pain, respectfully replied, "O revered Brahman, I appreciate your concern, but I have made a mistake that caused my Guru's distress. Only by fulfilling this penance as prescribed can I be purified. Please allow me to continue."

The Brahman smiled gently but said nothing more. As the king began his second prostration, something miraculous happened. Instead of feeling the searing heat of the copper plate, King Kulashekhara felt as though he was lying on a bed of soft, fragrant flowers. The burns from the first prostration vanished, and his skin was restored to its normal state.

The onlookers gasped in astonishment. They could not believe what they were witnessing. The intense heat of the copper plate had somehow turned into a cool, comforting flower bed beneath the king's body. They realized that a divine intervention had taken place.

The king, too, was astounded but continued his penance with deep gratitude in his heart. When he completed the 108th Sashtang Pranam, he rose to his feet, unscathed and with his sins cleansed. He turned to thank the Brahman who had spoken to him earlier, but the Brahman was nowhere to be seen. It was then that King Kulashekhara and the crowd understood that the Brahman was none other than Lord Jagannath Himself, who had come to protect His devotee.

The king, overwhelmed with emotion, immediately fell to his knees and offered his deepest gratitude to Lord Jagannath. "O Lord," he prayed, "you are the protector of your devotees. You have saved me from the consequences of my actions, and for that, I am eternally grateful. Please continue to guide me in my duties as king and in my devotion to you."

From that day forward, King Kulashekhara ruled his kingdom with even greater wisdom and compassion, knowing that Lord Jagannath was always watching over him. His story became a powerful testament to the Lord's mercy and the miraculous ways in which He protects those who serve Him with sincerity and devotion.

As the Guru spoke, a fly landed on the king Kulashekhara's forehead. Instinctively, the king removed the sacred dust, drawing the Guru's disapproval.

54

CHAPTER 7

LAKSHMI'S BLESSING

IN

DISGUISE

A TALE OF DEVOTION AND DIVINE JUSTICE

In the sacred temple of Puri, where Lord Jagannath, His brother Lord Balabhadra, and sister Goddess Subhadra are worshiped, Goddess Lakshmi, the divine consort of Lord Jagannath, also resides. Every Thursday, Goddess Lakshmi would leave the temple in disguise to visit her devotees and bless those who were devoted and sincere in their worship.

One Thursday, Goddess Lakshmi decided to visit a small village called Chandala, where the inhabitants were known for their simple and humble lives. Disguised as an old lady, Goddess Lakshmi wandered through the village, observing how the villagers lived. To her disappointment, she found that most of the villagers were careless in their daily routines.

They woke up late, neglected their cleanliness, and performed their chores in a dirty and disorganized manner. Goddess Lakshmi gently advised them to live in a more disciplined and pure way, but the villagers, unable to recognize her true identity, ignored her words and went about their day.

As Goddess Lakshmi continued her journey, she came across the house of a woman named Sriya Chandulini, who was different from the others in the village. Sriya Chandulini was a devout and pious woman who followed all the rituals with utmost sincerity. Her home was clean, her heart pure, and she performed her daily duties with devotion. Goddess Lakshmi was pleased with Sriya's dedication and invited herself inside her modest home.

Sriya Chandulini welcomed the old lady warmly and offered her whatever hospitality she could. Seeing Sriya's devotion, Goddess Lakshmi revealed her true form and blessed her with all the riches, happiness, and prosperity she could ever need. Sriya Chandulini was overwhelmed with gratitude, and after that Goddess Lakshmi returned to the temple, satisfied that she had found a worthy devotee.

However, upon her return to the temple, Goddess Lakshmi was met with resistance. Balabhadra, Lord Jagannath's elder brother, refused to allow her to enter. He was upset that she had visited Chandala village, a place inhabited by people of a lower caste, and argued that she had broken the temple's rules by doing so. Despite Lord Jagannath's attempts to explain that Goddess Lakshmi's love for her children extended to all, regardless of caste or status, Balabhadra remained adamant. He accused Lord Jagannath of favoring his wife and demanded that she be kept out of the temple.

Frustrated and hurt by Balabhadra's words, Lord Jagannath reluctantly agreed that Goddess Lakshmi could not enter the temple. But Goddess Lakshmi, being the goddess of wealth and sustenance, decided to teach the brothers a lesson. She declared that since they did not want her, she would withdraw her blessings, and they would have to fend for themselves. "Let's see who will feed you now," she said, "You can either eat from my hands or wander for food for 12 years."

As soon as Goddess Lakshmi left, Balabhadra and Lord Jagannath entered the temple, only to find that the kitchen was in complete disarray. The pots were broken, the fires unlit, and there was no food to be found. They rushed to the storeroom, but it too was empty. Desperate and hungry, the brothers decided to disguise themselves as Brahmins and go begging for food.

They went from door to door, asking for alms, but no one offered them anything. They wandered for hours, their hunger and thirst growing unbearable.

Eventually, they reached a Sarovar (lake) and decided that if they could not find food, they would at least drink some water. But as they approached the Sarovar (lake), they were shocked to find that it had dried up completely.

Exhausted and with nowhere else to go, the brothers reluctantly made their way to Chandala village, the very place Goddess Lakshmi had visited. They reached Sriya Chandulini's house and, still in disguise, asked her for alms. Recognizing the Brahmins as Lord Jagannath and Lord Balabhadra, Sriya Chandulini invited them inside and offered to cook a meal for them.

However, the brothers insisted on cooking the food themselves. Sriya Chandulini provided them with the ingredients, and then Balabhadra instructed Lord Jagannath to start cooking while he went to take a bath. But when Lord Jagannath tried to light the stove, the fire wouldn't catch. Frustrated and tired, he waited for brother Balabhadra to return, who came back without having bathed because the Sarovar (lake) was dry.

Seeing their plight, Sriya Chandulini offered to cook the meal for them. Too exhausted to refuse, the brothers agreed. As they sat down to eat, they were astonished by the taste of the food. It was as if the meal had been prepared by Goddess Lakshmi herself, just as it was in the temple.

Lord Jagannath turned to Sriya Chandulini and asked, "This food tastes exactly like the offerings made by Goddess Lakshmi in the temple. How is this possible?"

Sriya Chandulini smiled and revealed the truth. "My Lord, you are correct. It is indeed Goddess Lakshmi who prepared this meal for you in my humble home."

Realizing their mistake, Lord Balabhadra felt a deep sense of remorse. He understood that his actions had caused unnecessary suffering, and that Goddess Lakshmi's love and care extended beyond the confines of the temple. He had wronged the divine mother, and now it was time to seek her forgiveness.

The brothers immediately set out to find Goddess Lakshmi. They found her sitting by herself, still hurt by their actions. Lord Balabhadra fell at her feet and begged for her forgiveness, admitting that he had made a grave error. Lord Jagannath too joined him, asking Goddess Lakshmi to return to the temple.

Moved by their sincere repentance, Goddess Lakshmi forgave them and returned to the temple, restoring everything to its proper order. The kitchen was once again filled with abundance, the fires were lit, and the storerooms were overflowing with food. The brothers learned a valuable lesson: that the divine mother's love is unconditional and knows no boundaries, whether of caste, status, or temple walls.

From that day on, Lord Balabhadra and Lord Jagannath treated Goddess Lakshmi with the utmost respect and reverence, understanding that without her blessings, even the gods would go hungry. And so, the story of Mother Lakshmi's journey to Chandala village and the lesson she taught became a cherished tale, reminding everyone of the importance of humility, devotion, and the boundless love of the divine mother.

Goddess Lakshmi blessed Sriya Chandulini for her devotion and hospitality.

CHAPTER 8

THE MIRACULOUS PILLOW

Sutapa Saha

PARMESHTHI'S GIFT TO LORD JAGANNATH

Parmeshthi was a devoted follower of Lord Jagannath, living in Delhi. Despite being a hunchback and considered unattractive by society, he was renowned for his exceptional skills as a tailor. His craftsmanship was so exquisite that even the Mughal kings would seek out his services to stitch their royal garments and accessories.

One day, the Mughal king entrusted Parmeshthi with a special task. He handed him a piece of fine silk cloth, brought from a distant land, and asked him to create two pillow covers from it. Parmeshthi, honored by the king's request, accepted the task eagerly. He carefully measured, cut, and stitched the silk, creating the most beautiful pillow covers he had ever made.

As he held one of the completed pillows in his hands, Parmeshthi was struck by the sheer beauty and richness of the silk. The texture was so fine, and the craftsmanship so delicate, that he felt a deep yearning in his heart. He thought to himself, "Such a beautiful and precious piece of cloth deserves to touch the divine feet of Lord Jagannath. How wonderful it would be if this pillow could be used in the service of the Lord during the Rath Yatra in Puri."

The Rath Yatra, or the Festival of Chariots, was being celebrated in Puri at that very moment. On that day, known as Panhandi Vijay, the deities of Lord Jagannath, Lord Balabhadra, and Goddess Subhadra are ceremoniously placed on the grand chariots. As the pandas (temple priests) lifted the deities, they would place pillows beneath the Lord's feet for support. Parmeshthi, lost in his thoughts and deep devotion, closed his eyes and imagined Lord Jagannath's feet resting on the very pillow he had stitched. In his mind's eye, he could see the cotton from the pillow filling the air as it floated around, creating a beautiful and enchanting scene.

When Parmeshthi opened his eyes, he found that one of the pillows was missing. He searched everywhere but could not find it. Realizing that his sincere devotion had led to the pillow being accepted by Lord Jagannath, Parmeshthi was both overjoyed and anxious. He knew he had to tell the truth to the Mughal king, even if it meant risking punishment.

When the king asked for the pillow covers, Parmeshthi handed him the one he had and explained the miraculous disappearance of the other. He told the king about his deep devotion to Lord Jagannath and how, in his heart, he had offered the pillow to the Lord. He explained that, in response, the Lord had accepted his offering, and the pillow was now with Lord Jagannath in Puri.

The Mughal king was skeptical. He couldn't believe that a pillow stitched in Delhi could have made its way to Puri in such a miraculous manner. Accusing Parmeshthi of lying, the king ordered him to be imprisoned until he could prove his innocence.

That night, Parmeshthi prayed earnestly to Lord Jagannath, pleading for help. As he fell asleep, the Lord appeared in his dream and assured him, "Do not worry, Parmeshthi, I will take care of everything." As soon as Lord Jagannath touched him in the dream, Parmeshthi felt a transformation within himself. When he awoke, he discovered that his hunchback was gone, and he had become a handsome man, radiating with the Lord's grace.

The same night, the Mughal king also had a dream. In it, Lord Jagannath appeared before him and confirmed that Parmeshthi had spoken the truth. The Lord told the king that the pillow was indeed in Puri and that Parmeshthi's devotion was pure and sincere.

The next morning, the king summoned Parmeshthi from the prison. When Parmeshthi entered, the king was astounded by his appearance. The hunchback tailor was now a handsome, upright man, and the king immediately recognized the truth of his dream. He understood that Parmeshthi's devotion had indeed moved the Lord to intervene personally.

Filled with awe and respect, the Mughal king fell at Parmeshthi's feet and asked for his forgiveness. He praised Parmeshthi's unwavering devotion, acknowledging that Lord Jagannath himself had come to protect his devotee. From that day on, Parmeshthi was not only honored for his skill as a tailor but also revered for his deep devotion to Lord Jagannath.

The story of Parmeshthi and the miraculous pillow became a legend, reminding everyone of the power of true devotion and the boundless grace of Lord Jagannath, who watches over and protects his devotees, no matter where they are.

During Rath Yatra, Parmeshthi envisioned Lord Jagannath's feet on his stitched pillow, as cotton floated magically, filling the air with devotion, beauty, and divine grace.

72

CHAPTER 9

THE LOCKED DOORS

OF

PURI

Sutapa Saha

ODIAN ACHARYA'S JOURNEY FROM DOUBT TO DEVOTION

Odian Acharya, a renowned scholar from Mithila, was well-versed in the scriptures and revered for his knowledge. His intellect had made him proud, and though he had heard tales of the divine grace of Lord Jagannath, he found it hard to believe that merely visiting and having *darshan* (a sacred sight) of the Lord could relieve one from the suffering of earthly existence. Amused and skeptical, he decided to test the validity of these claims by visiting the Jagannath Temple in Puri.

With a heart filled with doubt and a mind clouded by pride, Odian Acharya made his way to the sacred city of Puri. Upon his arrival, he approached the grand temple of Lord Jagannath, eager to see if the divine stories he had heard held any truth. However, as he stood before the temple, something unexpected happened—the doors to the sanctum where Lord Jagannath resided did not open.

Perplexed, Odian Acharya thought it was merely a coincidence. He decided to try again the next day, confident that the doors would open. Yet, when he returned to the temple, the same thing happened.

.The priests and devotees attempted to open the doors, but despite their best efforts, the doors remained tightly shut. The people of Puri, who were accustomed to the daily rituals and prayers, were growing increasingly concerned.

The head priest, realizing that something unusual was happening, decided to meditate and seek guidance from Lord Jagannath. In his meditation, the Lord spoke to him, revealing the reason behind the locked doors. "I will not open my doors as long as a skeptic remains in Puri," Lord Jagannath said. "This person harbors doubt in his heart and does not have faith in me. His pride as a scholar blinds him to the truth."

The head priest, troubled by this revelation, asked the Lord to identify the person who was causing this disturbance. The Lord revealed that it was none other than Odian Acharya from Mithila. "As long as he stays in Puri with his heart full of doubt, I shall not open my doors," Lord Jagannath declared.

When the head priest came out of his meditation, he immediately ordered a search for Odian Acharya. The priests found him and confirmed his identity. With folded hands, the head priest approached Odian Acharya and humbly requested him to leave Puri. The scholar, surprised and confused, asked for an explanation.

The head priest recounted the Lord's words, explaining that Lord Jagannath had refused to open the temple doors because of Odian Acharya's lack of faith and his overwhelming pride in his scholarly achievements. The realization struck Odian Acharya like a lightning bolt. He understood that his pride and skepticism had kept him from experiencing the divine grace of Lord Jagannath.

Overcome with remorse, Odian Acharya rushed to the temple. Standing before the locked doors, he raised his hands in surrender and began to pray fervently. Tears streamed down his face as he acknowledged his mistake and begged for forgiveness. With a heart full of genuine repentance, he cried out to the Lord, thanking him for shattering his pride and revealing the truth.

As Odian Acharya's prayers filled the air, a miraculous event took place. The heavy wooden doors of the temple, which had remained closed for days, slowly creaked open. The temple priests and devotees watched in awe as the doors parted, revealing the resplendent form of Lord Jagannath. The air was thick with the divine presence, and everyone present could feel the Lord's grace enveloping them.

Odian Acharya fell to his knees, overwhelmed by the sight before him. The Lord had not only forgiven him but had also granted him the *darshan* that countless devotees yearned for. The scholar's heart, once filled with pride, was now brimming with devotion and gratitude.

From that day on, Odian Acharya became a changed man. His encounter with Lord Jagannath had transformed him, filling his heart with unwavering faith. He returned to Mithila, not just as a scholar, but as a devotee who had experienced the mercy of the Lord first hand. He spread the story of Lord Jagannath's grace far and wide, reminding everyone that true wisdom comes not from pride, but from humility and faith in the divine.

The story of Odian Acharya and Lord Jagannath became a cherished tale in Puri, a testament to the power of faith and the boundless compassion of Lord Jagannath, who patiently guides even the most doubtful hearts towards the light of devotion.

Odian Acharya's sincere repentance opened the temple
doors, revealing Lord Jagannath's grace, filling the air with
awe and devotion.

Sutapa Saha

CHAPTER 10

THE LORD WITH AN ELEPHANT TRUNK

Sutapa Saha

.

HOW LORD JAGANNATH FULFILLED GANAPATI BHAT'S DEVOTION

Ganapati Bhat, a devout worshiper of Lord Ganesha, lived in Karnataka. His devotion to Lord Ganesha was unwavering, and he spent much of his time reading scriptures and engaging in spiritual practices. One day, while studying a sacred text, he came across a passage that described Lord Jagannath as the *Param Brahma*—the Supreme Being. The scripture also stated that by having *darshan* (a sacred sight) of the *Param Brahma*, one could attain *mukti*—liberation or oneness with the Lord.

For Ganapati Bhat, *mukti* meant merging with the divine, becoming one with the Lord in eternal bliss. Intrigued by this idea, he resolved to visit Puri and have *darshan* of Lord Jagannath, believing that this would lead to his liberation.

In those days, there were no vehicles to make the journey easier, so Ganapati Bhat set out on foot, determined to reach Puri. He walked for days, asking people along the way for directions. His journey was long and arduous, but his devotion and desire for liberation kept him moving forward.

As he continued his journey, Ganapati Bhat encountered a group of travelers. He asked them where they were coming from, and they replied that they had just visited Puri and had *darshan* of Lord Jagannath. This puzzled Ganapati Bhat, for according to his understanding, having *darshan* of the *Param Brahma* should result in *mukti*—yet these travelers were still alive and on their way back home.

Perplexed and somewhat troubled, Ganapati Bhat continued on his journey, hoping to find answers. Along the way, he met an old man who was actually Lord Jagannath in disguise. The old man noticed Ganapati Bhat's troubled expression and asked him why he seemed so disturbed. Ganapati Bhat introduced himself and explained his doubts and concerns.

The old man smiled kindly and said, "Lord Jagannath fulfills the wishes of every devotee who prays to him with full devotion. If someone asks for *bhakti* (devotion), he grants them *bhakti*. If someone asks for *mukti*, he grants them *mukti*. Each devotee can approach him in their own way, and the Lord blesses them according to their wishes."

This explanation eased Ganapati Bhat's doubts to some extent, but he still felt the need to continue his journey and experience the truth for himself.

Eventually, Ganapati Bhat arrived in Puri and made his way to the Jagannath Temple. He stood at the gate and had his first *darshan* of Lord Jagannath from a distance. However, nothing happened; he did not feel the liberation he had been seeking. Slightly disheartened, he decided to stay another day and try again.

The next day was Snana Purnima also known as Deva Snana Purnima, a special occasion when Lord Jagannath is brought outside the Sri Mandir for a ceremonial bath. Ganapati Bhat eagerly awaited the moment, hoping that this would be the experience that would bring him *mukti*. But when he saw the deity, he was disappointed. He had imagined Lord Jagannath to have an elephant trunk like his beloved Lord Ganesha. Disappointed, he turned to leave.

Just as he was about to depart, a temple priest, known as a panda, hurried towards him with an urgent message. "Lord Jagannath has sent me to call you back," the panda said. "The Lord has promised that this time you will have *darshan* in the way you desire."

Intrigued and filled with a renewed sense of hope, Ganapati Bhat returned to the place where Lord Jagannath was being bathed. As he gazed upon the deities, he was amazed to see that they all appeared with elephant trunks, just like Lord Ganesha.

Overwhelmed with joy and devotion, Ganapati Bhat fell to his knees in reverence. In that moment, he felt his spirit leaving his body and merging with the divine essence of Lord Jagannath.

Through the spiritual sky, Ganapati Bhat found himself in a divine realm—an actual spiritual Jagannath Puri. Before him stood the Lord in his *Chaturbhuja* (four-armed) form, radiating divine light and love. Ganapati Bhat, filled with overwhelming bliss, performed *sashtang pranam* (a full prostration) before the Lord. He realized that his wish for *mukti* had been fulfilled in the most profound way possible.

With tears of joy streaming down his face, he praised the Lord, chanting "Jai Jagannath! Jai Jagannath!" over and over again. His heart was filled with gratitude as he realized that Lord Jagannath had granted him the ultimate gift—liberation and eternal union with the divine.

The story of Ganapati Bhat and his journey to Puri became a cherished tale, illustrating the boundless grace of Lord Jagannath, who fulfills the wishes of his devotees in ways they cannot even imagine. It is a testament to the power of devotion and the Lord's willingness to reveal his true form to those who seek him with a pure heart.

Ganapati Bhat saw the deities with elephant trunks, amazed and filled with hope by Lord Jagannath's divine, Ganesha-like appearance.

www.ingramcontent.com/pod-product-compliance
Lightning Source LLC
Chambersburg PA
CBHW031452150726
47990CB00007B/2727